SUPER SANDCASTLE™
Creature Features

What Has Paws?

Mary Elizabeth Salzmann

ABDO
Publishing Company

Published by ABDO Publishing Company, 8000 West 78th Street, Edina, Minnesota 55439. Copyright © 2008 by Abdo Consulting Group, Inc. International copyrights reserved in all countries. No part of this book may be reproduced in any form without written permission from the publisher. Super SandCastle™ is a trademark and logo of ABDO Publishing Company.

Printed in the United States.

Credits
Editor: Pam Price
Content Developer: Nancy Tuminelly
Cover and Interior Design and Production: Mighty Media
Photo Credits: Corbis Images, JupiterImages Corporation, Photodisc, Shutterstock, Steve Wewerka

Library of Congress Cataloging-in-Publication Data

Salzmann, Mary Elizabeth, 1968-

  What has paws? / Mary Elizabeth Salzmann.

    p. cm. -- (Creature features)

  ISBN 978-1-59928-869-7

  1. Foot--Juvenile literature. I. Title.

  QL950.7.S24 2007

  591.47'9--dc22

                    2007012010

Super SandCastle™ books are created by a team of professional educators, reading specialists, and content developers around five essential components— phonemic awareness, phonics, vocabulary, text comprehension, and fluency— to assist young readers as they develop reading skills and strategies and increase their general knowledge. All books are written, reviewed, and leveled for guided reading, early reading intervention, and Accelerated Reader® programs for use in shared, guided, and independent reading and writing activities to support a balanced approach to literacy instruction.

About SUPER SANDCASTLE™

Bigger Books for Emerging Readers
Grades PreK–3

Created for library, classroom, and at-home use, Super SandCastle™ books support and engage young readers as they develop and build literacy skills and will increase their general knowledge about the world around them. Super SandCastle™ books are part of SandCastle™, the leading PreK–3 imprint for emerging and beginning readers. Super SandCastle™ features a larger trim size for more reading fun.

Let Us Know
Super SandCastle™ would like to hear your stories about reading this book. What was your favorite page? Was there something hard that you needed help with? Share the ups and downs of learning to read. We want to hear from you! Send us an e-mail.

sandcastle@abdopublishing.com

Contact us for a complete list of SandCastle™, Super SandCastle™, and other nonfiction and fiction titles from ABDO Publishing Company.

www.abdopublishing.com • 8000 West 78th Street Edina, MN 55439 • 800-800-1312 • 952-831-1632 fax

A paw is a kind of animal foot. Paws have several toes with a nail or claw on each toe.

Cheetahs have paws.

Cheetahs can run faster than any other animal. Their paws have hard pads and claws that don't retract. This gives them extra traction to help them run fast.

Raccoons have paws.

Raccoons have long toes on their front paws, which help them grip their food when they eat. They can also open doors and trash cans.

Wolves have paws.

Wolf paws are very large, which gives them support on snow. They also have stiff hairs around the pads of their feet. These hairs provide warmth and traction on ice.

Giant pandas have paws.

Giant pandas have five toes on each paw. They also have extra-long wrist bones that help them grip things. These special bones act kind of like thumbs.

Geckos have paws.

There are special tiny hairs on a gecko's toe pads that let it cling to surfaces such as leaves and walls. Geckos can even walk on ceilings.

Cats have paws.

Most cats have five toes on their front paws and four toes on their back paws. But some cats have extra toes. They are called polydactyl cats.

Koalas have paws.

A koala's paws each have two toes opposite the other three toes. This helps them grip things such as tree branches and food. Koalas eat eucalyptus leaves.

Rabbits have paws.

Unlike the paws of most mammals, rabbit paws don't have pads on the bottom. Rabbits drum their long back paws on the ground to warn other rabbits of danger.

Orangutans have paws.

Like all primates, orangutans have front paws that are very similar to human hands. They have four fingers with an opposable thumb. They even leave fingerprints.

What would you do if you had paws?

MORE CREATURES
THAT HAVE PAWS

lion

bear

dog

squirrel

otter

GLOSSARY

eucalyptus - an Australian tree that is grown for its oil and wood.

fingerprint - the mark made by the ridges in the skin on a fingertip.

mammal - a warm-blooded animal that is covered with hair and, in the female, produces milk to feed the young.

pad - a thick, fleshy cushion on the bottom of an animal's paw.

polydactyl - having more than the normal number of fingers or toes.

primate - a mammal with developed hands and feet, a large brain, and a short nose, such as a human, ape, or monkey.

retract - to pull back in.

support - to hold up.

traction - the friction that helps something grip a surface.

unlike - different or not alike.